The Big Africa
Companion Journal

Which biomes are in Africa?

Fill the biome map with a different color for each biome.
You can use your Africa Biome Cards or Puzzle as a reference.

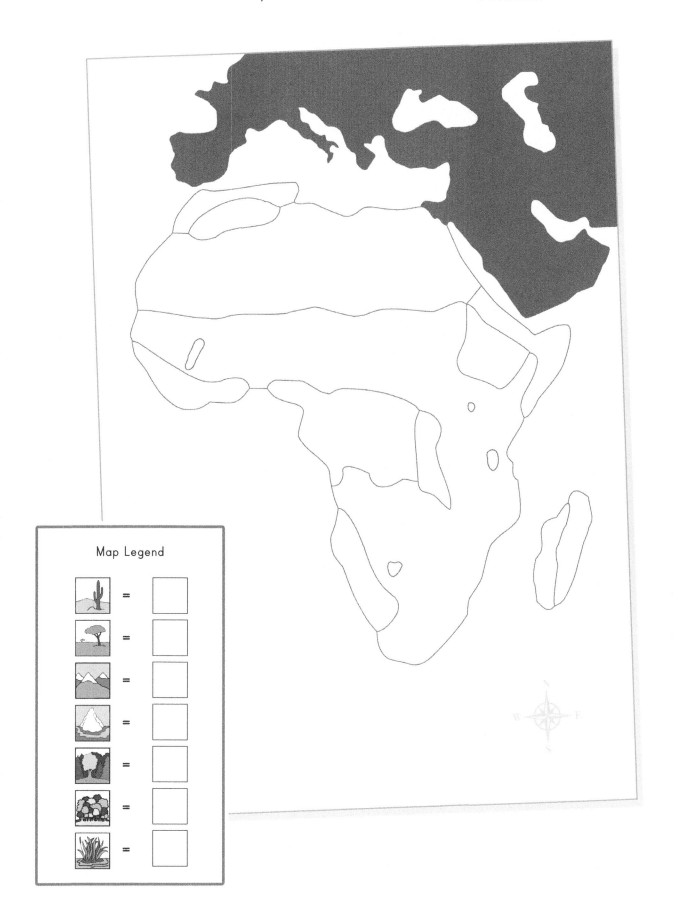

Map Legend

NAME _____

BIOME

It eats...

It lives in...

Its body is covered in...

It also...

NAME _____

BIOME

It eats...

It lives in...

Its body is covered in...

It also...

NAME _____

BIOME

It eats...

It lives in...

Its body is covered in...

It also...

NAME _____

BIOME

It eats...

It lives in...

Its body is covered in...

It also...

NAME _____

BIOME

It eats...

It lives in...

Its body is covered in...

It also...

NAME _____

BIOME

It eats...

It lives in...

Its body is covered in...

It also...

NAME _____

BIOME

It eats...

It lives in...

Its body is covered in...

It also...

NAME _____

BIOME

It eats...

It lives in...

Its body is covered in...

It also...

NAME _____

BIOME

It grows in...

I wonder...

NAME _____

BIOME

NAME _____

BIOME

NAME _____

BIOME

Made in the USA
Middletown, DE
29 April 2023

29710620R00044